Power and Politics in the Global South: A Comparative Study for Students

Oleg Petrov

Copyright © [2023]

Title: Power and Politics in the Global South: A Comparative Study for Students

Author's: Oleg Petrov.

2

This book was printed and published by [Publisher's: Oleg Petrov] in [2023]

ISBN:

TABLE OF CONTENTS

Chapter 10: Conclusion and Future Perspectives 85

Chapter 1: Introduction to Power and Politics in the Global South

Understanding Power and Politics

In the complex landscape of global affairs, power and politics play a central role in shaping the destinies of nations. As students of comparative politics, it is essential to comprehend the intricate dynamics of power and politics to navigate through the complexities of the global South. This subchapter aims to provide a comprehensive understanding of power and politics, shedding light on their interplay and impact on societies.

To begin with, power can be defined as the ability to influence others and bring about desired outcomes. In the political realm, power is often concentrated in the hands of governing bodies or individuals. However, power can also be distributed across various actors, such as interest groups, social movements, or even ordinary citizens. Understanding the different sources and forms of power is crucial to comprehend how decisions are made and policies are implemented in any society.

Politics, on the other hand, refers to the processes through which power is acquired, exercised, and contested. It encompasses the activities and strategies employed by individuals, groups, and institutions to gain and maintain power. Politics goes beyond the formal structures of government; it encompasses the broader social, economic, and cultural contexts that shape power dynamics. By studying politics, students can unravel the mechanisms through which power is wielded and its implications for governance and policy-making.

To analyze power and politics in the global South, a comparative approach is essential. Comparing different countries and regions allows us to discern similarities and differences in power structures, political systems, and policy outcomes. Through case studies and empirical evidence, students can explore how historical legacies, socio-economic factors, and cultural dimensions influence power and politics in diverse contexts.

Moreover, understanding power and politics in the global South necessitates an examination of power relations between states and the international system. The dynamics of power in the global arena are shaped by geopolitical interests, economic dependencies, and historical imbalances. Students must grasp these power dynamics to comprehend how countries in the global South navigate the complex web of international relations.

In conclusion, the subchapter on understanding power and politics provides students of comparative politics with a solid foundation to comprehend the intricate dynamics of power and politics in the global South. By delving into the sources and forms of power, the processes of politics, and the role of power in international relations, students can gain a nuanced understanding of how societies and countries operate. This knowledge will equip them to critically analyze and contribute to the field of comparative politics, allowing for a better comprehension of the challenges and opportunities faced by the global South.

The Importance of Comparative Politics in Developing Countries

Introduction:

In the global south, where developing countries face unique political challenges, comparative politics plays a crucial role in understanding and analyzing political systems. This subchapter explores the significance of comparative politics in developing countries, highlighting its relevance for students studying comparative politics.

Understanding Political Systems:

Comparative politics provides a framework for understanding the diversity of political systems across developing countries. By examining similarities and differences, students can gain insight into the evolution, functioning, and challenges of these systems. It enables them to grasp the complexities of political dynamics and the factors that shape them.

Promoting Democracy and Good Governance:

One of the primary concerns in developing countries is the establishment and consolidation of democratic systems. Comparative politics allows students to examine different democratic models, their successes, and failures. It helps identify the elements necessary for the promotion of democratic values, institutions, and practices. Through comparative analysis, students can also evaluate the effectiveness of various governance mechanisms, such as accountability, transparency, and participation.

Addressing Inequality and Social Justice:

Developing countries often grapple with rampant inequality and social injustices. Comparative politics enables students to explore the relationship between political systems and social issues. By comparing policies, institutions, and ideologies, students can better understand the impact of political choices on poverty, education, healthcare, and other social concerns. This knowledge equips them to advocate for more inclusive and equitable societies.

Analyzing Political Economy:

The economic development of developing countries is closely intertwined with their political systems. Comparative politics allows students to investigate the interaction between politics and the economy. They can analyze how different political systems shape economic policies, resource distribution, and patterns of development. This understanding is crucial for formulating effective strategies to address economic challenges and foster sustainable growth.

Conflict Analysis and Resolution:

Developing countries often experience internal conflicts, ethnic tensions, and political instability. Comparative politics equips students with the tools to analyze and understand the causes and dynamics of these conflicts. By studying case studies, they can identify successful conflict resolution mechanisms and learn from past mistakes. This knowledge is invaluable for students interested in pursuing careers in diplomacy, peacebuilding, or international relations.

Conclusion:

The study of comparative politics in developing countries is of paramount importance for students interested in understanding the complexities of political systems and contributing to positive change. By examining similarities and differences, students can gain insights into the challenges faced by these countries and propose innovative solutions. Comparative politics empowers students to promote democracy, address social injustices, analyze political economies, and contribute to conflict resolution. As future leaders, policymakers, or scholars, students in comparative politics have the opportunity to make a lasting impact on the global south.

Scope and Objectives of the Book

Welcome to "Power and Politics in the Global South: A Comparative Study for Students!" This book is specifically designed for students interested in the field of comparative politics. In this subchapter, we will explore the scope and objectives of this book, providing you with a comprehensive overview of what to expect throughout your reading journey.

The primary scope of this book is to analyze and understand the dynamics of power and politics in the Global South. The Global South refers to countries in Africa, Asia, Latin America, and the Caribbean, which are often characterized by their unique historical, economic, and social contexts. By focusing on these regions, we aim to shed light on the diverse political systems, processes, and institutions that shape the political landscape in these areas.

Our objective is to provide students with a comparative framework to analyze and critically evaluate the political systems of the Global South. Through a comprehensive study of various case studies, theories, and empirical evidence, this book aims to enhance your understanding of the similarities, differences, and complexities of political systems in these regions.

Throughout this book, you will explore topics such as colonialism, post-colonialism, democratization, authoritarianism, social movements, and political parties. We will examine how historical legacies, economic factors, culture, and social dynamics influence political power structures and decision-making processes in the Global South.

By the end of this book, you will have gained a deep understanding of the unique challenges, opportunities, and dynamics that shape politics in the Global South. You will be equipped with the knowledge and analytical skills necessary to critically evaluate political systems and processes in these regions, as well as to compare them with other parts of the world.

Whether you are a student of political science, international relations, or simply interested in understanding the complexities of global politics, "Power and Politics in the Global South: A Comparative Study for Students" will provide you with a solid foundation to navigate the intricacies of comparative politics in the Global South. Get ready to embark on an enlightening journey that will broaden your horizons and deepen your understanding of power and politics in the Global South.

Overview of Chapters

In "Power and Politics in the Global South: A Comparative Study for Students," we embark on an enlightening journey through the intricate world of comparative politics in the Global South. This book is specifically designed for students, providing an accessible and comprehensive exploration of power dynamics and political systems across regions such as Africa, Asia, Latin America, and the Middle East. By examining these regions through a comparative lens, students will gain a nuanced understanding of the unique challenges and opportunities faced by countries in the Global South.

This subchapter, "Overview of Chapters," serves as a road map to guide students through the subsequent chapters of the book. It provides a brief overview of the key topics and themes that will be explored, offering valuable insight into the rich tapestry of political landscapes in the Global South.

Chapter 1 delves into the theoretical foundations of comparative politics, introducing students to various frameworks and approaches used to analyze power and politics in different contexts. By understanding these theoretical underpinnings, students will be equipped to critically examine and compare political systems across the Global South.

Chapter 2 focuses on the historical legacies that have shaped contemporary politics in the Global South. It examines the impact of colonialism, independence movements, and post-colonial struggles for power, highlighting how historical events continue to shape political dynamics in these regions.

Chapter 3 explores the diverse forms of governance in the Global South, ranging from authoritarian regimes to democracies. Through comparative case studies, students will examine the factors that contribute to the persistence or transition of different governance systems, shedding light on the complexities of political power.

Chapter 4 delves into the role of political parties and electoral systems in the Global South. Students will analyze the challenges faced by political parties in representing diverse interests and the impact of electoral systems on political stability and representation.

Chapter 5 investigates the influence of social movements and civil society organizations in shaping political landscapes. By examining various movements, such as labor movements, feminist movements, and environmental movements, students will gain insight into the ways in which social mobilization can challenge or reinforce existing power structures.

Chapter 6 explores the interplay between power, politics, and socioeconomic development in the Global South. Students will examine the role of state actors, international organizations, and economic policies in shaping development outcomes, highlighting the complexities of the relationship between power and progress.

By navigating through these chapters, students will develop a comprehensive understanding of the diverse political systems and power dynamics in the Global South. This book aims to equip students with the knowledge and analytical tools necessary to critically analyze and compare political systems across regions, fostering a deeper appreciation for the intricate tapestry of power and politics in the Global South.

Chapter 2: Theoretical Frameworks in Comparative Politics

Introduction to Comparative Politics

Welcome to the subchapter on "Introduction to Comparative Politics" from the book "Power and Politics in the Global South: A Comparative Study for Students." In this section, we will delve into the fascinating world of comparative politics, providing you with a solid foundation to understand and analyze political systems across the globe.

What is Comparative Politics?

Comparative politics is a field of study that explores the similarities and differences between various political systems, institutions, and processes. By comparing different countries and regions, we gain valuable insights into how politics operates and the factors that shape governance, policies, and power dynamics.

Why Study Comparative Politics?

Studying comparative politics is essential for students interested in understanding the complexities of the global political landscape. It allows us to examine the impact of historical, economic, cultural, and social factors on political systems and outcomes. By analyzing different cases, we can identify patterns, trends, and challenges that transcend borders, enabling us to develop a comprehensive understanding of political phenomena.

Key Concepts in Comparative Politics

To navigate the field of comparative politics effectively, it is crucial to grasp some key concepts. This subchapter will introduce you to important terms such as political systems, regime types, ideologies, political institutions, political culture, and policy-making processes. Understanding these concepts will provide you with a solid framework to analyze and compare different political systems.

Approaches in Comparative Politics

Comparative politics utilizes various approaches to study political systems. This subchapter will familiarize you with the major theoretical frameworks, including institutionalism, rational choice theory, and cultural approach. By exploring these approaches, you will gain a deeper understanding of how scholars examine and explain political phenomena.

Regional Focus: The Global South

In this book, we particularly focus on the Global South, comprising countries in Africa, Asia, Latin America, and the Middle East. The Global South faces unique challenges and opportunities, such as post-colonial legacies, democratization processes, economic development, and social movements. By examining political systems within this context, we can gain insights into the dynamics of power and politics in diverse settings.

Conclusion

In this subchapter, we have provided you with an introduction to the field of comparative politics, its significance, key concepts, and approaches. By studying comparative politics, you will develop critical thinking skills and analytical tools that will enable you to understand and engage with the complexities of politics in the global arena. So, let's embark on this exciting journey to explore the rich tapestry of political systems and power dynamics worldwide.

Classical Approaches to Comparative Politics

In the realm of comparative politics, understanding the various theoretical perspectives is crucial for students seeking to delve into the complexities of political systems across the globe. This subchapter aims to provide a comprehensive overview of the classical approaches to comparative politics, highlighting the key theories and concepts that have shaped the field.

One of the foundational theories explored in this subchapter is the structural-functional approach. This approach focuses on analyzing the functions and structures of political systems, emphasizing how different institutions and processes work together to maintain stability and order. Students will gain insights into the functionalist perspective on political institutions, such as legislatures, executives, and judiciaries, and how they contribute to the overall functionality of a political system.

Additionally, this subchapter delves into the historical institutionalism approach, which emphasizes the importance of historical factors and path dependency in shaping political outcomes. By understanding how past events and institutions influence present-day politics, students will have a better grasp of the complexities of comparative politics. Historical institutionalism sheds light on how specific political systems evolve and adapt, providing valuable insights into the political dynamics of the global South.

Another classical approach covered is the rational choice theory, which focuses on individual actors and their decision-making processes. Students will explore how rational actors, such as politicians or voters, make choices based on their self-interests and preferences. By analyzing the incentives and constraints that shape political behavior, students can gain a deeper understanding of political outcomes and the dynamics of power.

Furthermore, this subchapter introduces the sociological approach to comparative politics, which emphasizes the role of social forces and structures in shaping political systems. Students will explore how factors such as social class, ethnicity, and religion influence political behavior and the distribution of power. By examining the social dimensions of political systems, students can gain valuable insights into the challenges and opportunities faced by societies in the global South.

Overall, this subchapter on classical approaches to comparative politics provides students with a solid foundation for understanding the complexities of political systems. By exploring theories such as structural-functionalism, historical institutionalism, rational choice, and sociology, students will develop the analytical tools necessary to critically analyze and compare political systems across the global South. With this knowledge, students will be well-equipped to navigate the intricacies of comparative politics and contribute to the study and understanding of power and politics in the contemporary world.

Modern Approaches to Comparative Politics

In recent years, the field of comparative politics has witnessed a profound transformation due to the emergence of modern approaches that have revolutionized the way we study and understand politics in the global South. These approaches have allowed students of comparative politics to delve deeper into the complexities of political systems, institutions, and processes, shedding light on the unique challenges and opportunities faced by countries in the global South.

One of the key modern approaches to comparative politics is the focus on institutions and their impact on political outcomes. Institutions, such as political parties, legislatures, and judiciaries, play a crucial role in shaping the political dynamics of a country. By analyzing the design, functioning, and effectiveness of these institutions, students can gain a comprehensive understanding of how power is distributed, how policies are formulated, and how political stability or instability is maintained in different contexts.

Another important modern approach is the emphasis on social movements and civil society organizations. These grassroots movements have become catalysts for change, challenging existing power structures and advocating for social, economic, and political reforms. By studying these movements, students can gain insights into the mobilization of citizens, the dynamics of collective action, and the impact of social movements on policy-making processes.

Furthermore, the modern approaches to comparative politics have also incorporated a focus on political economy. This interdisciplinary perspective examines how economic factors, such as wealth distribution, globalization, and market forces, shape political processes and outcomes. By analyzing the relationship between economics and politics, students can understand the underlying drivers of political decision-making and the impact of economic policies on different social groups.

Moreover, gender and identity politics have emerged as critical areas of study within comparative politics. These approaches examine how gender, ethnicity, religion, and other identity markers influence political behavior, representation, and policy-making. By analyzing the intersectionality of identities and politics, students can gain a deeper understanding of power dynamics and inequalities within societies.

Overall, modern approaches to comparative politics have expanded the scope and depth of our understanding of political systems in the global South. By incorporating institutional analysis, social movements, political economy, and identity politics, students can now explore the complexities and nuances of comparative politics in a more comprehensive and interdisciplinary manner. These approaches not only enhance our academic knowledge but also equip us with the analytical tools necessary to critically engage with the challenges and opportunities faced by countries in the global South.

Application of Theoretical Frameworks in the Global South

The Global South, comprising developing and underdeveloped nations, has long been a subject of interest and study for scholars in the field of comparative politics. The region's unique socio-economic, historical, and cultural contexts have necessitated the development of theoretical frameworks that better capture the dynamics of power and politics in these countries. In this subchapter, we will explore the application of theoretical frameworks in the Global South, shedding light on the complexities and nuances that shape political systems.

One prominent theoretical framework used in the Global South is the Dependency Theory, which analyzes the relationship between developed and developing nations. This framework examines how external forces, such as colonialism and economic exploitation, have perpetuated underdevelopment in the Global South. By understanding the historical and structural factors that have contributed to this dependency, students can critically assess power dynamics and political challenges faced by these nations.

Another theoretical framework extensively employed in the Global South is Postcolonial Theory. This framework emphasizes the impact of colonialism on the political, economic, and cultural landscapes of these countries. It explores how colonial legacies have shaped power structures, identities, and development trajectories. By applying this framework, students can gain a nuanced understanding of the struggles faced by postcolonial nations in their quest for political autonomy and socio-economic progress.

Furthermore, the subchapter will delve into the relevance of the State-Civil Society Relations framework in the Global South. It explores the intricate interactions between state institutions and non-state actors, such as social movements, grassroots organizations, and NGOs. This framework offers students insights into the role of civil society in shaping political outcomes, advocating for marginalized groups, and fostering democratic processes in the Global South.

Lastly, the subchapter will touch upon the applicability of the Gender and Power framework in the Global South. Recognizing the unique challenges faced by women in these societies, this framework examines how gender intersects with power dynamics. Students will gain an understanding of the gendered nature of politics, the impact of patriarchal norms, and the efforts made to address gender inequality and promote women's empowerment in the Global South.

By exploring these theoretical frameworks, students will be equipped with the analytical tools to comprehend the complex dynamics of power and politics in the Global South. They will develop a critical perspective on the historical, social, and economic factors that have shaped these nations, empowering them to engage in informed discussions and contribute to the field of comparative politics.

Chapter 3: Historical Context of Power and Politics in the Global South

Colonial Legacy and its Impact on Politics

Introduction

The legacy of colonialism has had a profound impact on the political systems of many countries in the Global South. This subchapter explores the lasting effects of colonial rule on politics and governance, providing students with a comprehensive understanding of the complexities and challenges faced by these nations.

Historical Background

To comprehend the impact of colonialism on politics, it is crucial to delve into the historical context. European powers, such as Britain, France, Spain, and Portugal, colonized vast territories in Africa, Asia, and Latin America during the 18th and 19th centuries. These colonial powers imposed their own political systems, institutions, and ideologies, often exploiting local resources for their own benefit.

Political Institutions and Systems

One major consequence of colonialism is the persistence of political institutions and systems inherited from the colonial period. Many former colonies adopted Western-style governance structures, including parliamentary systems, bureaucracies, and legal frameworks. These institutions, while providing some stability, also perpetuated power imbalances, as they were designed to serve the interests of the colonizers rather than the local populations.

Ethnic and Religious Divisions

Colonial powers often exacerbated ethnic and religious divisions within their colonies, employing a strategy of divide and rule to maintain control. These divisions persist today, leading to political instability and conflicts in many post-colonial nations. Students will gain insight into the challenges of managing diverse ethnic and religious groups within the framework of a unified political system.

Economic Dependency and Inequality

Colonialism established patterns of economic dependency, with colonies serving as sources of raw materials and cheap labor for the colonizers' industries. This legacy of economic exploitation has contributed to persistent inequality and underdevelopment in many countries. Students will examine the impact of these economic disparities on political dynamics, including the rise of populist movements and the challenges of implementing effective governance.

National Identity and Post-Colonial Politics

The struggle to define national identity following independence is a recurring theme in post-colonial politics. Students will explore how the legacy of colonialism has shaped national narratives and the quest for self-determination. The subchapter will also examine the role of post-colonial leaders in shaping political systems and ideologies, sometimes perpetuating authoritarianism or fostering democratic transitions.

Conclusion

Understanding the colonial legacy and its impact on politics is essential for students studying comparative politics in the Global South. This subchapter provides a comprehensive analysis of the historical, institutional, economic, and social factors that continue to shape political landscapes in these regions. By gaining insights into the complexities of post-colonial politics, students will be better equipped to analyze and engage with the challenges and opportunities facing these nations on their path towards sustainable development and democratic governance.

Post-Colonial Challenges in the Global South

Post-colonial challenges in the Global South have had a profound impact on the political landscape of countries across Africa, Asia, and Latin America. In this subchapter, we will explore the various obstacles and struggles that these nations have faced in the wake of their colonial past, and how they continue to shape their political systems today. This discussion is particularly relevant to students studying comparative politics, as it provides a deeper understanding of the unique challenges faced by countries in the Global South.

One of the key challenges faced by post-colonial nations is the legacy of political instability and weak institutions left behind by colonial powers. Colonial rule often resulted in the exploitation of resources, enforced cultural assimilation, and the marginalization of indigenous populations. As a result, newly independent states in the Global South had to grapple with building strong political institutions from scratch, while also addressing internal divisions and power struggles.

Furthermore, economic challenges have plagued many post-colonial nations. The extraction of resources during colonial rule often led to the underdevelopment of local industries and economies, leading to a heavy reliance on the export of primary commodities. This dependency on a single industry, coupled with unequal trade relations with former colonial powers, has hindered economic diversification and sustainable development.

Additionally, post-colonial countries have had to confront the issue of identity and nationalism. The artificial boundaries drawn by colonial powers often ignored ethnic, religious, and linguistic differences, leading to persistent tensions and conflicts. These nations have had to grapple with questions of national identity and forge a sense of unity among diverse populations, while also accommodating demands for regional autonomy and self-determination.

Furthermore, the Global South has faced challenges in establishing democratic governance and ensuring the protection of human rights. Many post-colonial states experienced authoritarian rule, military coups, and one-party systems that stifled political freedoms and civil liberties. Transitioning to democratic systems has been a complex process, often marked by power struggles and a lack of institutional capacity.

Despite these challenges, the Global South has also witnessed significant progress and resilience. Many countries have successfully transitioned to stable democracies, achieved economic growth, and improved social indicators. The subchapter will not only highlight the challenges but also explore the strategies employed by different countries to overcome these obstacles, emphasizing the importance of context-specific approaches.

In conclusion, understanding the post-colonial challenges in the Global South is crucial for students studying comparative politics. It sheds light on the complex dynamics that have shaped the political systems in these countries and provides valuable insights into the diverse strategies employed to navigate these challenges. By examining the historical context and contemporary realities, students can develop a deeper appreciation for the unique experiences of the Global South and the ongoing efforts to address the legacies of colonialism.

Nationalism and State Building in Developing Countries

In the realm of comparative politics, one of the crucial aspects to understand is the relationship between nationalism and state building in developing countries. This subchapter delves into this intricate interplay, shedding light on the dynamics, challenges, and implications of nationalism for state formation in the Global South.

Nationalism, as an ideology, has historically been a potent force in shaping the political landscape of developing countries. It has played a pivotal role in mobilizing the masses, uniting diverse ethnic and cultural groups, and providing a sense of identity and purpose. Nationalism often emerges as a response to colonialism, oppression, or socio-economic disparities, fueling aspirations for self-determination and sovereignty.

In the context of state building, nationalism can be both a unifying and divisive force. For instance, it can foster a sense of belonging and loyalty to the nation-state, leading to the consolidation of power and the establishment of strong institutions. This sense of national identity can serve as a binding force, promoting social cohesion and stability. However, nationalism can also lead to exclusionary policies, discrimination against minority groups, and the suppression of dissenting voices, which can undermine the democratic fabric of a state.

Developing countries face unique challenges in their state-building processes, often characterized by weak institutions, ethnic tensions, and socio-economic disparities. Nationalism can either exacerbate these challenges or provide a framework for addressing them.

Understanding the role of nationalism in state building is therefore crucial for students of comparative politics.

This subchapter explores case studies from various regions of the Global South, highlighting the diverse experiences and outcomes of nationalism in state formation. It examines the impact of nationalist movements, the role of charismatic leaders, and the influence of external factors such as globalization and imperialism. By analyzing these cases, students gain a comprehensive understanding of the complexities and nuances of nationalism in the context of developing countries.

Moreover, this subchapter critically examines the limitations and potential pitfalls of nationalism as a tool for state building. It explores how nationalism can be manipulated by elites for their own political agendas, leading to the marginalization of certain groups and the perpetuation of authoritarian regimes. By analyzing these drawbacks, students develop a nuanced understanding of the challenges that arise when nationalism becomes a dominant force in state formation.

Ultimately, this subchapter provides students with a comprehensive understanding of the intricate relationship between nationalism and state building in developing countries. By examining case studies, exploring theoretical frameworks, and critically analyzing the implications of nationalism, students gain the necessary tools to analyze and evaluate the complexities of comparative politics in the Global South.

Globalization and its Effects on Power Dynamics in the Global South

In recent decades, globalization has emerged as a defining force in shaping the dynamics of power in the global South. As students of comparative politics, it is crucial to understand the multifaceted impacts of globalization on the political landscape of developing nations. This subchapter aims to provide a comprehensive analysis of globalization's effects on power dynamics in the global South, offering valuable insights for students interested in comparative politics.

Globalization, broadly defined as the increasing interconnectedness and interdependence of nations, has had far-reaching consequences on the political structures and power dynamics of the global South. One of the primary effects has been the erosion of state sovereignty. As countries open up their economies to global markets, they often become subject to the demands and influence of international organizations and powerful transnational corporations. This has significantly diminished the autonomy of nation-states, as decisions on economic policies and development strategies are increasingly dictated by external forces.

Furthermore, globalization has led to the emergence of new actors in the global South. Non-state actors, such as multinational corporations, non-governmental organizations, and civil society groups, have gained significant influence in shaping political agendas and policies. Their ability to mobilize resources, exert pressure on governments, and influence public opinion has reshaped power dynamics, challenging traditional power structures dominated by the state.

Globalization has also brought both opportunities and challenges for the global South. On one hand, it has provided avenues for economic growth and technological advancements, enabling countries to participate in global trade networks and attract foreign direct investment. However, it has also exacerbated existing inequalities within and between nations, as the benefits of globalization are not evenly distributed. This has led to social unrest and political instability, with marginalized groups and vulnerable populations demanding their fair share of the globalization dividends.

Understanding the intricate nexus between globalization and power dynamics is crucial for students of comparative politics. By examining case studies from various regions of the global South, this subchapter will delve into the complexities of how globalization has transformed the political landscape, reshaping power relations, challenging traditional hierarchies, and offering both opportunities and challenges for developing nations.

In conclusion, globalization has significantly impacted power dynamics in the global South, reshaping the political landscape and challenging traditional power structures. This subchapter aims to provide students with a nuanced understanding of these effects, drawing on comparative case studies to illuminate the complexities of globalization's influence on the political dynamics of developing nations. By engaging with this topic, students will be equipped with valuable insights to navigate the complexities of power and politics in the global South.

Chapter 4: Institutions and Governance in the Global South

Political Systems in Developing Countries

In today's globalized world, understanding the political systems of developing countries is of utmost importance. These countries, often referred to as the Global South, face unique challenges and opportunities in their pursuit of political stability and economic development. This subchapter aims to provide students with a comprehensive overview of the political systems in developing countries, equipping them with the necessary knowledge to analyze and compare different political systems within this context.

One key aspect to consider is the diversity of political systems within developing countries. While some countries may have democratic systems in place, others might be governed by authoritarian regimes or hybrid models. This diversity arises from various historical, cultural, and socio-economic factors that shape the political landscape in each country. Students will learn to critically evaluate the strengths and weaknesses of different political systems, considering factors such as representation, accountability, and the protection of human rights.

Furthermore, the subchapter will delve into the challenges faced by developing countries in establishing and maintaining political stability. Issues such as corruption, weak institutions, and political violence often hinder the progress of these nations. By examining case studies from different regions, students will gain a deeper understanding of the complex dynamics that influence political systems in developing countries.

The subchapter will also explore the role of international actors in shaping the political systems of developing countries. Students will learn how global powers, international organizations, and non-governmental organizations influence political processes, often with conflicting interests. This understanding will enable students to critically analyze the impact of external actors on the political development of these nations.

Additionally, the subchapter will highlight the importance of inclusive political systems in promoting sustainable development in developing countries. Students will explore the concept of political inclusion, examining how the participation of marginalized groups, including women and ethnic minorities, can contribute to more equitable and just societies. The subchapter will provide examples of successful initiatives and policies that promote political inclusivity, encouraging students to think critically about potential solutions to address existing inequalities.

Overall, this subchapter aims to empower students with a comprehensive understanding of political systems in developing countries. By studying comparative politics within the context of the Global South, students will develop the analytical skills necessary to critically evaluate political systems, identify challenges, and propose potential solutions for promoting political stability and sustainable development in these nations.

Comparative Analysis of Democratic and Authoritarian Regimes

In the realm of comparative politics, the study of democratic and authoritarian regimes serves as a fundamental cornerstone. Understanding the differences between these two forms of governance is crucial for students aiming to comprehend the dynamics of power and politics in the global south. This subchapter aims to provide a comprehensive analysis of democratic and authoritarian regimes, shedding light on their defining characteristics, strengths, weaknesses, and implications for society.

Democratic regimes, characterized by popular participation, transparency, and accountability, have long been hailed as the epitome of political systems that safeguard individual liberties and foster collective decision-making. Such regimes prioritize citizen engagement through mechanisms like free and fair elections, the rule of law, and protection of human rights. Students will explore the rich tapestry of democratic institutions, including the separation of powers, independent judiciary, and vibrant civil society, which serve as checks and balances against excessive concentration of power.

On the other hand, authoritarian regimes represent a stark departure from democratic principles. Concentration of power in the hands of a single individual or a small elite group defines these systems. Students will delve into the mechanisms employed by authoritarian regimes to maintain control, such as censorship, surveillance, and suppression of dissent. Understanding the nuances of authoritarianism is crucial, given its prevalence in many parts of the global south, and its impact on society, human rights, and economic development.

Through a comparative lens, students will critically analyze the strengths and weaknesses of democratic and authoritarian regimes. Democracies, with their emphasis on political pluralism and open discourse, excel in fostering innovation, economic growth, and social stability. However, they are not without challenges, including the potential for gridlock, corruption, and the manipulation of democratic processes. Conversely, authoritarian regimes may provide efficiency and stability in the short term, but at the expense of individual liberties, human rights, and long-term political resilience.

By studying the comparative analysis of democratic and authoritarian regimes, students will gain a deeper understanding of the complex tapestry of power and politics in the global south. Armed with this knowledge, they will be better equipped to critically analyze the strengths and weaknesses of different political systems, evaluate their implications for society, and contribute to the ongoing debates surrounding governance and democracy in the modern era.

Role of Bureaucracy and Judiciary in the Global South

In the realm of comparative politics, understanding the role of bureaucracy and judiciary is crucial in comprehending power dynamics in the Global South. Bureaucracy refers to the administrative system responsible for implementing government policies, while the judiciary is the branch of government entrusted with interpreting and upholding the law. Together, these institutions play a vital role in shaping governance, democracy, and the overall political landscape in the Global South.

One significant aspect of bureaucracy in the Global South is its historical legacy. Many countries in this region were former colonies, and their administrative systems were inherited from their colonizers. This colonial legacy profoundly influenced the bureaucratic structures, norms, and practices in the Global South. Consequently, bureaucracy in these countries often exhibits characteristics such as centralization, red tape, and corruption. Understanding this legacy helps students comprehend the challenges and complexities faced by bureaucratic institutions in the Global South.

Furthermore, the judiciary in the Global South plays a crucial role in safeguarding the rule of law and ensuring accountability. However, it is important to recognize that the judiciary in these countries faces numerous challenges, including political interference, lack of resources, and corruption. These challenges can undermine the independence and effectiveness of the judiciary, making it difficult for it to act as a check on executive power. By examining specific case studies and examples, students can gain a deeper understanding of the complexities surrounding judicial independence and the rule of law in the Global South.

Moreover, the role of bureaucracy and judiciary in the Global South extends beyond domestic affairs. These institutions also play a crucial role in shaping international relations. Bureaucrats and judges participate in international forums, negotiate agreements, and represent their countries' interests on the global stage. Understanding the influence and participation of the bureaucracy and judiciary in international affairs provides students with a comprehensive understanding of the power dynamics at play in the Global South.

In conclusion, comprehending the role of bureaucracy and judiciary in the Global South is essential for students of comparative politics. By exploring the historical legacy, challenges faced, and their impact on both domestic and international affairs, students can gain a deeper understanding of the power dynamics and governance in the Global South.

Challenges and Reforms in Governance Systems

In the ever-changing landscape of global politics, governance systems play a crucial role in shaping societies and managing the affairs of nations. However, these systems are not immune to challenges that arise from various sources, including internal and external factors. This subchapter explores the key challenges faced by governance systems in the global south and the reforms that are being implemented to address these issues.

One of the major challenges faced by governance systems in the global south is corruption. Corruption undermines the legitimacy of governments, erodes public trust, and hampers socio-economic development. This subchapter delves into the causes and consequences of corruption and highlights the efforts being made to combat this pervasive problem. It also examines the role of civil society organizations, media, and international actors in fostering transparency and accountability.

Another significant challenge is the issue of political instability. Many countries in the global south have experienced political upheavals, including coups, civil wars, and social unrest. This subchapter explores the causes of political instability and analyzes the impact on governance systems. It also examines the role of democratic reforms, such as inclusive governance and participatory decision-making, in promoting stability and preventing conflicts.

Furthermore, the subchapter discusses the challenges posed by globalization and the need for governance systems to adapt to an interconnected world. It explores issues related to migration, trade, and environmental sustainability, and their implications for governance. It also highlights the importance of regional cooperation and international partnerships in addressing these challenges.

Reforms in governance systems are essential to overcome these challenges and ensure effective and responsive governance. The subchapter provides examples of successful governance reforms from different countries in the global south. It examines initiatives such as decentralization, e-governance, and anti-corruption measures, and assesses their impact on governance outcomes.

As students of comparative politics, understanding the challenges and reforms in governance systems in the global south is crucial. This subchapter equips students with the knowledge and analytical tools to critically assess governance systems and contribute to discussions on policy reform. It encourages students to explore case studies, engage in debates, and propose innovative solutions to improve governance in their respective countries and regions.

In conclusion, this subchapter highlights the challenges faced by governance systems in the global south and the ongoing efforts to implement reforms. By exploring these issues, students gain a deeper understanding of the complexities of governance and the importance of effective governance systems in promoting inclusive and sustainable development.

Word count: 299 words

Chapter 5: Civil Society and Social Movements in the Global South

Importance of Civil Society in Developing Countries

Title: Importance of Civil Society in Developing Countries

Introduction:

In developing countries, the role of civil society cannot be underestimated in fostering democratic governance, social progress, and sustainable development. This subchapter aims to shed light on the significance of civil society in the context of developing nations. By examining the interplay between power and politics, we can understand how civil society acts as a catalyst for positive change. This knowledge is particularly relevant for students of comparative politics, who seek to comprehend the dynamics of governance and social transformation.

The Role of Civil Society:

Civil society encompasses non-governmental organizations (NGOs), community-based groups, grassroots movements, and other voluntary associations. These organizations act as a bridge between the state and its citizens, representing diverse interests and advocating for marginalized groups. In developing countries, where institutions may be weak or corrupt, civil society plays a crucial role in promoting transparency, accountability, and citizens' participation.

Promoting Democracy and Human Rights:

Civil society acts as a watchdog, monitoring the government's actions and holding it accountable for its policies and decisions. Through advocacy campaigns and public awareness programs, civil society organizations empower citizens to exercise their democratic rights, such as freedom of expression and association. By amplifying marginalized voices and demanding inclusive governance, civil society helps strengthen democratic processes and protect human rights in developing countries.

Addressing Social Issues:

One of the primary functions of civil society in developing countries is to address social issues such as poverty, gender inequality, environmental degradation, and health disparities. NGOs and community-based organizations play a vital role in providing social services, advocating for policy reforms, and promoting sustainable development practices. By engaging with local communities and mobilizing resources, civil society organizations can fill gaps left by the government and promote social justice.

Facilitating Development and Aid:

Civil society acts as a bridge between international development agencies and local communities in developing countries. Through their knowledge of local contexts and needs, civil society organizations facilitate effective development programs and ensure that aid reaches the intended beneficiaries. By promoting transparency and accountability in aid delivery, civil society enhances the impact of development initiatives and reduces the risk of corruption.

Conclusion:

Understanding the importance of civil society in developing countries is crucial for students of comparative politics. By recognizing the role civil society plays in fostering democratic governance, advocating for human rights, addressing social issues, and facilitating development, students can gain insights into the dynamics of power and politics in the global South. As future leaders and policymakers, students can actively engage with civil society organizations to promote inclusive and sustainable development in developing countries.

Role of NGOs and Activist Groups in the Global South

In recent years, the Global South has witnessed a surge in the activities of non-governmental organizations (NGOs) and activist groups. These organizations and groups play a crucial role in shaping the political landscape and addressing various social, economic, and environmental issues. This subchapter explores the significance of NGOs and activist groups in the Global South, focusing on their impact on politics and their contributions to social change.

NGOs and activist groups in the Global South have emerged as important actors in promoting democracy, human rights, and social justice. They act as a counterforce to the power dynamics dominated by governments and multinational corporations. By advocating for marginalized groups, they challenge the existing power structures and demand accountability from those in authority.

One of the key roles played by NGOs and activist groups is their ability to give voice to the voiceless. They represent the interests and concerns of marginalized communities, including indigenous peoples, women, and ethnic minorities. Through their advocacy and lobbying efforts, they raise awareness about human rights violations, environmental degradation, and economic inequalities.

Furthermore, NGOs and activist groups often act as catalysts for social change. They mobilize communities, organize protests, and engage in grassroots campaigns to raise awareness and bring about policy reforms. Their activities range from providing healthcare and education to rural communities, fighting against corruption, and promoting sustainable development.

In addition to their advocacy work, NGOs and activist groups in the Global South also contribute to capacity building and empowerment. They provide training and resources to local communities, enabling them to participate in decision-making processes and become active citizens. By empowering individuals and communities, they foster a sense of ownership and resilience, ultimately leading to sustainable development.

However, it is important to recognize that the role of NGOs and activist groups in the Global South is not without challenges. They often face resistance from governments and powerful interest groups who perceive them as threats to their authority. Moreover, limited funding and resources hinder their ability to sustain their activities and make a lasting impact.

In conclusion, NGOs and activist groups in the Global South play a crucial role in promoting democracy, human rights, and social justice. They give voice to marginalized communities, mobilize for social change, and contribute to capacity building and empowerment. Despite the challenges they face, their collective efforts have the potential to shape political landscapes and bring about positive transformations in the Global South. As students of comparative politics, it is essential to understand and appreciate the role of NGOs and activist groups in driving political change and addressing social issues in the Global South.

Social Movements and their Impact on Power Dynamics

In the realm of politics, power dynamics play a crucial role in shaping societies and determining the course of governance. One significant force that has the potential to challenge and reshape these power dynamics is social movements. This subchapter will delve into the concept of social movements and their profound impact on power dynamics, particularly in the context of the Global South.

Social movements can be defined as collective efforts by a group of individuals who come together to advocate for social or political change. These movements arise due to a shared dissatisfaction with existing power structures and aim to challenge the status quo. Throughout history, social movements have played a pivotal role in bringing about significant shifts in power dynamics, leading to transformative change in societies.

The Global South, comprising developing nations, is particularly fertile ground for social movements due to the prevalent socio-economic disparities and political inequalities. In this subchapter, we will explore the diverse social movements that have emerged in the Global South, ranging from labor movements and women's rights movements to environmental movements and anti-colonial movements. By examining these movements, students will gain a comprehensive understanding of the various strategies employed by social activists to challenge power dynamics and advocate for change.

Furthermore, this subchapter will analyze the impact of social movements on power dynamics. Students will learn how social movements can disrupt established power structures, forcing governments and political elites to address pressing social issues. By amplifying the voices of marginalized groups and challenging entrenched hierarchies, social movements can lead to the redistribution of power and the advancement of social justice.

Additionally, this subchapter will critically analyze the limitations and challenges faced by social movements in the Global South. Students will explore the complexities surrounding the sustainability and effectiveness of these movements, taking into account factors such as state repression, co-optation, and internal divisions. By examining both the successes and failures of social movements, students will gain a nuanced understanding of their potential and limitations in reshaping power dynamics.

Overall, this subchapter aims to equip students with a comprehensive understanding of social movements and their impact on power dynamics in the Global South. By examining real-world case studies and engaging in critical analysis, students will develop the necessary tools to comprehend and navigate the complex world of comparative politics.

Case Studies of Successful and Failed Social Movements

In the fascinating realm of politics, social movements have played a crucial role in shaping the course of history. From the fight for women's suffrage to the struggle for civil rights, these movements have mobilized masses, challenged power structures, and brought about significant changes in society. This subchapter delves into the analysis of successful and failed social movements, offering valuable insights into the dynamics of power and politics in the Global South.

By examining case studies of both successful and failed social movements, students of comparative politics can gain a deeper understanding of the factors that contribute to the triumph or downfall of such movements. These case studies shed light on the strategies employed, the challenges faced, and the outcomes achieved by different social movements across various regions of the Global South.

One successful case study to consider is the African National Congress (ANC) in South Africa. The ANC's decades-long struggle against apartheid is a testament to the power of organized resistance and collective action. Through a combination of nonviolent protests, international pressure, and strategic alliances, the ANC successfully dismantled the oppressive apartheid regime, leading to the establishment of a democratic and inclusive South Africa.

On the other hand, the failed social movement of the Arab Spring serves as a cautionary tale. Initially hailed as a wave of democratic change, the Arab Spring movements faced numerous challenges, including internal divisions, lack of leadership, and repression from authoritarian governments. Despite the initial momentum, many of these movements failed to achieve their desired outcomes, resulting in political instability and in some cases, even further repression.

By studying these and other case studies, students can analyze the factors that contribute to the success or failure of social movements. Factors such as leadership, organization, popular support, external pressures, and the ability to adapt strategies are all crucial elements that shape the trajectory of social movements. Understanding these dynamics can help students develop a more nuanced understanding of power and politics in the Global South.

Moreover, these case studies highlight the interconnectedness of social movements across different regions. Students can explore the influence of transnational networks, global media, and international organizations on the outcomes of social movements. This analysis encourages students to think beyond the borders of individual nations and understand the broader global context in which social movements operate.

In conclusion, the study of successful and failed social movements provides a valuable lens through which students of comparative politics can examine power and politics in the Global South. By analyzing case studies, students can gain insights into the strategies, challenges, and outcomes of different social movements, enabling them to develop a more nuanced understanding of the dynamics at play. These case studies also emphasize the importance of global interconnectedness and the role of external factors in shaping the fate of social movements.

Chapter 6: Political Economy and Development in the Global South

Economic Systems in Developing Countries

In the global arena, developing countries play a critical role in shaping the economic landscape. The economic systems implemented in these nations greatly influence their social and political dynamics. This subchapter aims to provide an insightful analysis of the various economic systems found in developing countries, focusing on their impact on power and politics.

One of the predominant economic systems in developing countries is state-led capitalism. In this system, the government assumes a significant role in guiding and controlling economic activity. State-led capitalism often involves extensive state ownership of key industries and strategic planning to promote economic growth. This approach allows governments to exert influence over the distribution of resources and shape national development priorities. However, it also raises concerns about corruption and inefficiency, as concentrated power can lead to exploitation and favoritism.

Another economic system observed in developing countries is market liberalism. Market liberal economies emphasize free markets, private property rights, and minimal government intervention. This system aims to stimulate economic growth through competition and innovation. While market liberalism can lead to economic prosperity, it also exacerbates social inequality and leaves vulnerable populations marginalized. The power dynamics in such systems are often influenced by powerful business interests, who can exert substantial influence over political processes.

In contrast, some developing countries adopt mixed economies, combining elements of both state-led capitalism and market liberalism. This approach attempts to strike a balance between government intervention and market forces. Mixed economies allow for strategic state intervention in critical sectors while also encouraging private enterprise and competition. The power dynamics in mixed economies can be complex, as governments and private entities negotiate and compete for influence.

The economic systems in developing countries have significant implications for power and politics. They shape the distribution of wealth, access to resources, and opportunities for social mobility. These factors, in turn, influence political dynamics, including elections, policy-making, and the balance of power within society.

Understanding the economic systems in developing countries is crucial for students of comparative politics. It allows them to analyze and comprehend the complexities of power and politics in these regions. By examining the strengths and weaknesses of various economic systems, students can gain a deeper understanding of the challenges and opportunities faced by developing nations, as well as the potential for political reform and social change.

Role of International Institutions in Shaping Economic Policies

The Role of International Institutions in Shaping Economic Policies

In today's interconnected world, the role of international institutions in shaping economic policies cannot be overstated. These institutions play a pivotal role in promoting economic development, stability, and cooperation among nations. In the global south, where various political systems and economic structures coexist, understanding the influence of international institutions is crucial for students studying comparative politics.

International institutions such as the International Monetary Fund (IMF), World Bank, and World Trade Organization (WTO) have been instrumental in shaping economic policies across the global south. These institutions provide financial assistance, technical expertise, and policy advice to member countries, helping them navigate economic challenges and pursue sustainable development.

One of the key roles of international institutions is to promote economic stability. They work closely with governments to address macroeconomic imbalances, such as high inflation, budget deficits, and currency fluctuations. Through programs like structural adjustment, these institutions offer financial support in exchange for policy reforms aimed at promoting fiscal discipline, market liberalization, and privatization. By enforcing these policies, international institutions aim to create an environment conducive to economic growth and attract foreign investment.

Moreover, international institutions also play a crucial role in fostering global trade. The WTO, for instance, sets the rules for international trade and resolves disputes between member countries. By ensuring a level playing field and reducing trade barriers, the WTO facilitates economic integration and promotes fair competition. This is particularly relevant for students studying comparative politics, as trade policies and agreements significantly impact a country's economic development and political dynamics.

International institutions also contribute to sustainable development by addressing issues such as poverty reduction, environmental protection, and social inclusiveness. Through various initiatives and projects, these institutions strive to promote inclusive growth, reduce income inequality, and safeguard the environment. By integrating social and environmental considerations into economic policies, they help create a more equitable and sustainable future for the global south.

In conclusion, international institutions play a crucial role in shaping economic policies in the global south. Their influence extends beyond financial support, as they provide technical expertise, policy advice, and promote economic stability and cooperation among nations. By studying the role of these institutions, students of comparative politics can develop a comprehensive understanding of the complex interplay between power, politics, and economic development in the global south.

Challenges and Opportunities for Economic Development

In today's interconnected and rapidly changing world, economic development is a critical concern for countries in the Global South. This subchapter explores the various challenges and opportunities that these nations face in their pursuit of economic growth and prosperity. By understanding these dynamics, students of comparative politics can gain valuable insights into the complexities of power and politics in the Global South.

One of the major challenges for economic development in the Global South is the persistence of poverty and inequality. Many countries in this region struggle with high levels of poverty, which hampers their ability to invest in education, healthcare, and infrastructure. Additionally, income inequality often exacerbates social tensions and can lead to political instability. Students studying comparative politics can delve into the root causes of these challenges, such as colonial legacies, weak institutions, and unequal distribution of resources.

Another key challenge is the reliance on commodity exports. Many countries in the Global South depend heavily on the export of primary commodities such as oil, minerals, and agricultural products. This dependence exposes them to external shocks, such as fluctuations in global commodity prices, which can destabilize their economies. Students can explore the political implications of this reliance, including the potential for corruption, resource curse, and the need to diversify economic activities.

However, amidst these challenges lie numerous opportunities for economic development. The Global South is home to a young and growing population, which can serve as a valuable demographic dividend if harnessed effectively. Students can examine how policies that invest in education, skills training, and job creation can unlock the potential of this demographic dividend, driving economic growth and reducing poverty.

Furthermore, the Global South offers vast untapped markets and opportunities for trade and investment. As emerging economies continue to rise, there is a growing demand for goods and services, providing a chance for countries in the Global South to promote inclusive growth through trade and investment. Students can analyze the role of regional integration initiatives, such as the African Continental Free Trade Area or the Association of Southeast Asian Nations, in harnessing these opportunities.

In conclusion, this subchapter on challenges and opportunities for economic development is essential for students of comparative politics who seek to understand the power dynamics and political complexities in the Global South. By critically examining the challenges of poverty, inequality, reliance on commodity exports, and the opportunities presented by demographic dividends and expanding markets, students can gain a comprehensive understanding of the factors shaping economic development in this region. Armed with this knowledge, they can contribute to crafting effective policies and strategies that promote sustainable and inclusive economic growth in the Global South.

Case Studies of Successful and Struggling Economies in the Global South

In the ever-evolving world of politics and economics, the Global South has become a focal point for scholars and students. The Global South, comprising countries from Africa, Asia, and Latin America, has experienced various degrees of success and struggle in their economic endeavors. This subchapter aims to examine case studies of successful and struggling economies within the Global South, shedding light on the intricate relationship between power, politics, and economic development.

To comprehend the dynamics of successful economies, it is crucial to explore the case of South Korea. Once ravaged by the Korean War, South Korea transformed itself into a global economic powerhouse within a few decades. By implementing robust industrial policies, investing in education and technology, and fostering a culture of entrepreneurship, South Korea achieved remarkable economic growth and development. Analyzing this case study allows students to understand how political decisions and policies can shape a nation's economic trajectory positively.

On the other hand, the struggles faced by economies in the Global South are evident in the case of Zimbabwe. Once considered the breadbasket of Africa, Zimbabwe's economy experienced a severe downturn due to a combination of political instability, corruption, and mismanagement. Hyperinflation, land seizures, and lack of investor confidence have led to a significant decline in the country's economic prospects. Exploring the Zimbabwean case study provides students with an opportunity to analyze the impact of political factors on economic development and the consequences of policy failures.

Furthermore, this subchapter delves into the case of Brazil, highlighting its transition from economic instability to relative success. By implementing structural reforms, investing in social programs, and diversifying its economy, Brazil has managed to reduce poverty rates, attract foreign investment, and become an emerging economic power. Understanding Brazil's journey allows students to explore the role of political will, policy implementation, and social programs in achieving sustainable economic growth.

Lastly, the subchapter examines the struggles faced by Venezuela, once a prosperous nation with vast oil reserves. Political turmoil, corruption, and mismanagement have pushed the country into an economic crisis, marked by hyperinflation, scarcity of basic goods, and mass emigration. The Venezuelan case study serves as a cautionary tale for students, emphasizing the detrimental consequences of political instability and poor governance on an economy.

In conclusion, this subchapter on case studies of successful and struggling economies in the Global South offers students a comprehensive understanding of the interplay between power, politics, and economic development. By examining the experiences of South Korea, Zimbabwe, Brazil, and Venezuela, students gain valuable insights into the factors that contribute to economic success or failure. Armed with this knowledge, students can critically analyze and compare different political and economic systems, preparing them to navigate the complex world of comparative politics.

Chapter 7: Gender and Power in the Global South

Gender Inequality and its Impact on Politics

Introduction:

Gender inequality continues to be a persistent issue in many societies around the world, and its impact on the political arena cannot be overstated. This subchapter aims to shed light on the role of gender inequality in politics, discussing its manifestations, consequences, and potential solutions. By understanding the impact of gender inequality on politics, students of comparative politics can gain valuable insights into the complexities of power dynamics and the challenges faced by marginalized groups within society.

Manifestations of Gender Inequality in Politics: Gender inequality is often reflected in the underrepresentation of women in political institutions and decision-making bodies. Despite progress in recent decades, women continue to be significantly underrepresented in political leadership positions globally. This underrepresentation can be attributed to various factors, including gender stereotypes, cultural norms, and discriminatory practices that hinder women's political participation. Additionally, gender-based violence and harassment present significant barriers for women seeking to engage in politics, further perpetuating inequality.

Consequences of Gender Inequality in Politics: The consequences of gender inequality in politics are far-reaching and affect not only marginalized groups but society as a whole. The lack of diversity in political leadership hampers the development and implementation of inclusive policies that address the needs and concerns of all citizens. The absence of women's perspectives in decision-making processes limits the range of ideas and solutions, hindering progress towards gender equality and sustainable development. Moreover, gender inequality in politics reinforces social norms and power imbalances, perpetuating discrimination and exclusion in other spheres of life.

Solutions   and   Progress:
Efforts to address gender inequality in politics have gained momentum in recent years, with various initiatives and policies aimed at promoting women's political participation. Quota systems, for example, have been implemented in several countries to ensure a minimum representation of women in political positions. Additionally, grassroots movements and civil society organizations have played a crucial role in advocating for gender equality in politics and amplifying the voices of marginalized groups. Education and awareness campaigns have also been instrumental in challenging gender stereotypes and promoting equal opportunities for women in political leadership.

Conclusion:
Understanding the impact of gender inequality on politics is paramount for students of comparative politics, as it provides a comprehensive view of power dynamics and challenges in different societies. By recognizing the manifestations and consequences of gender inequality in politics, students can contribute to the development of more inclusive and equitable political systems. Efforts to address gender inequality in politics must continue, as greater gender representation and participation are vital for sustainable development and social progress in the global south and beyond.

Women's Political Participation in Developing Countries

In recent years, there has been a growing recognition of the importance of women's political participation in developing countries. The empowerment of women and their active involvement in decision-making processes are crucial for inclusive and sustainable development. This subchapter aims to explore the challenges and opportunities that women face in participating in politics in the Global South, with a specific focus on developing countries.

One of the major challenges that women encounter is the deep-rooted gender inequality prevalent in many societies. Traditional gender roles and stereotypes often limit women's access to education, economic opportunities, and political power. This hinders their ability to participate effectively in political processes. Moreover, cultural norms and societal expectations often discourage women from engaging in politics, viewing it as a domain exclusive to men.

However, despite these challenges, there have been significant strides towards enhancing women's political participation in developing countries. Various international organizations, governments, and civil society groups have been actively promoting gender equality and women's empowerment. Legal reforms have been implemented to ensure equal representation of women in political institutions. Quota systems, for example, have been adopted in some countries to guarantee a minimum percentage of women in decision-making positions.

Furthermore, women's political participation has proven to have numerous benefits for society as a whole. Research has shown that when women are involved in politics, there is a greater emphasis on social issues such as healthcare, education, and poverty reduction. Women's perspectives and experiences bring a unique and valuable contribution to policy-making processes. Moreover, increased women's political participation is associated with improved governance, reduced corruption, and enhanced democracy.

To promote women's political participation further, it is crucial to address the structural and cultural barriers that hinder their engagement. This requires comprehensive strategies that include education and awareness campaigns to challenge gender norms, capacity building programs to enhance women's leadership skills, and the creation of safe spaces for women to express their political aspirations. Additionally, fostering partnerships between governments, civil society organizations, and international actors is essential for sustained progress in this area.

In conclusion, women's political participation in developing countries is vital for inclusive and sustainable development. Despite the challenges they face, women have made significant strides in breaking down barriers and asserting their rightful place in political decision-making processes. By addressing the structural and cultural obstacles that hinder their engagement, societies can harness the full potential of women's participation and create a more equitable and prosperous future for all.

Empowerment and Challenges for Women in the Global South

In recent years, there has been a significant push for the empowerment of women in the Global South. As students of comparative politics, it is essential to understand the unique challenges faced by women in these regions and the efforts being made to address them.

The Global South encompasses countries in Africa, Asia, Latin America, and the Caribbean. While each of these regions has its own distinct culture and political landscape, they share common challenges when it comes to women's empowerment. Gender inequality, discrimination, and limited access to education and healthcare are some of the key issues faced by women in the Global South.

One of the most significant barriers to women's empowerment is the persistence of patriarchal norms and customs. These social norms often perpetuate gender roles that limit women's opportunities and participation in public life. However, numerous grassroots movements and organizations have emerged to challenge these norms and advocate for women's rights. These movements are crucial in raising awareness and pushing for policy changes that promote gender equality.

Education is another fundamental aspect of women's empowerment. In many parts of the Global South, girls face barriers to accessing education due to factors such as poverty, cultural beliefs, and early marriage. Lack of education limits their opportunities for economic independence and political participation. Efforts are being made by governments, NGOs, and international organizations to improve access to education for girls and provide training programs that enhance their skills and knowledge.

Furthermore, economic empowerment plays a vital role in advancing women's rights. In the Global South, women often face limited economic opportunities and are overrepresented in low-paying jobs. However, several initiatives have been implemented to promote women's entrepreneurship and financial inclusion. These initiatives aim to provide women with the necessary resources, training, and support to start their own businesses and achieve economic independence.

Despite these positive developments, women in the Global South continue to face significant challenges. Violence against women, including domestic violence, sexual assault, and trafficking, remains a critical issue. Governments and civil society organizations are working together to strengthen laws and institutions to combat gender-based violence and provide support services for survivors.

In conclusion, the empowerment of women in the Global South is a complex and ongoing process. Students of comparative politics must be aware of the unique challenges faced by women in these regions and the efforts being made to address them. By understanding these issues, we can contribute to the global movement for gender equality and work towards a more inclusive and just society for all.

Case Studies of Gender Equality Initiatives in the Global South

In recent years, the issue of gender equality has gained significant attention worldwide. While progress has been made in many regions, the Global South remains an area of concern in terms of achieving gender equality. This subchapter aims to explore case studies of gender equality initiatives implemented in various countries of the Global South, highlighting the challenges faced and the lessons learned.

One notable case study is India's Mahila Samakhya program, which translates to "Women's Equality" in English. This initiative, launched in the 1980s, aimed to empower rural women by providing them with education and opportunities for economic independence. The program successfully mobilized women's collectives, enabling them to engage in decision-making processes and challenge gender norms. The case study offers valuable insights into the importance of grassroots organizing and community participation in promoting gender equality.

Another case study focuses on Rwanda's gender quota system, which has been instrumental in promoting women's political representation. Following the devastating genocide in 1994, Rwanda implemented a constitutional provision that reserved 30% of parliamentary seats for women. This initiative has resulted in Rwanda having the highest percentage of women in parliament globally. The case study emphasizes the role of political will and legal mechanisms in advancing gender equality, especially in post-conflict societies.

Moving to Latin America, Brazil's Bolsa Família program showcases the intersectionality of poverty and gender inequality. This conditional cash transfer program provided financial assistance to low-income families, with a specific focus on women as the primary recipients. By targeting women, the initiative aimed to enhance their economic autonomy and decision-making power within the household. The case study highlights the importance of incorporating a gender perspective into poverty alleviation programs.

These case studies illustrate the diversity of gender equality initiatives in the Global South and shed light on the complexities involved in addressing this issue. They also provide valuable lessons for students studying comparative politics. Understanding the context-specific challenges and successes in different regions can contribute to a comprehensive understanding of the factors that influence gender equality.

Overall, this subchapter serves as a resource for students interested in comparative politics, enabling them to explore the dynamics of gender equality initiatives in the Global South. By examining these case studies, students can gain insights into the strategies, policies, and outcomes of gender equality initiatives, ultimately fostering a deeper understanding of power and politics in these regions.

Chapter 8: Conflict and Security in the Global South

Types of Conflict in Developing Countries

In the realm of comparative politics, it is essential to examine the various types of conflict that occur in developing countries. These conflicts, which arise due to a range of factors, can significantly shape the political landscape and have a profound impact on the lives of individuals within these nations. This subchapter aims to provide students with a comprehensive understanding of the different types of conflict prevalent in developing countries.

1. Ethnic and Religious Conflict: Developing countries often comprise diverse ethnic and religious groups, creating a potential source of tension. Ethnic and religious conflicts can arise due to historical grievances, competition for resources, or political manipulation. Students will explore case studies from countries such as Sudan, Nigeria, and Sri Lanka, examining the root causes and consequences of these conflicts.

2. Political Instability: Many developing countries experience political instability, characterized by frequent changes in government, coups, or civil unrest. This section will delve into the reasons behind political instability, including weak institutions, corruption, and power struggles. Students will analyze the impact of political instability on governance, economic development, and social cohesion.

3. Socioeconomic Conflict: Inequality, poverty, and social exclusion can give rise to socioeconomic conflict in developing countries. This subchapter will explore the causes and consequences of such conflicts,

including protests, strikes, and civil disobedience. Students will examine the role of class divisions, resource distribution, and economic policies in fueling socio-economic conflict.

4. Resource-based Conflict: Developing countries are often rich in natural resources, such as oil, diamonds, or minerals. Paradoxically, these resources can become a source of conflict rather than prosperity. This section will focus on resource-based conflicts, including resource nationalism, competition for control over resources, and the environmental consequences of resource extraction.

5. Secessionist Movements: Some developing countries experience secessionist movements, where certain regions or ethnic groups seek independence from the central government. Students will explore case studies such as Kashmir, Catalonia, and South Sudan, analyzing the causes, dynamics, and implications of these movements on state sovereignty and stability.

By examining these different types of conflict in developing countries, students will gain a deeper understanding of the complex political dynamics at play in the global South. Moreover, this knowledge will enable them to critically analyze the root causes of conflicts, evaluate potential solutions, and appreciate the interconnectedness between political power, resources, and social divisions in developing nations.

Through a comparative lens, students will be equipped with the necessary tools to navigate the complexities of global politics and contribute to the development of more inclusive and sustainable societies in the future.

Causes and Consequences of Conflict in the Global South

Introduction:

In the realm of comparative politics, understanding the causes and consequences of conflict in the Global South is of utmost importance. The Global South, a term that encompasses developing countries across Africa, Asia, and Latin America, has been marred by numerous conflicts throughout history. This subchapter aims to shed light on the underlying causes and far-reaching consequences of these conflicts, providing students with a comprehensive understanding of power dynamics and politics in this region.

Causes of Conflict in the Global South:

1. Colonial Legacy: Many conflicts in the Global South can be traced back to the colonial era. The arbitrary drawing of borders, the imposition of foreign political systems, and the exploitation of natural resources created deep-rooted divisions and grievances that persist to this day.

2. Ethnic and Religious Divisions: The Global South is characterized by its diverse ethnic, religious, and cultural makeup. These differences can often become a source of tension and conflict, as rival groups compete for resources, power, or ideological dominance.

3. Socioeconomic Inequality: Widespread poverty, limited access to education, and lack of economic opportunities contribute to social and economic disparities in the Global South. These inequalities can fuel social unrest and provide fertile ground for conflict to flourish.

Consequences of Conflict in the Global South:

1. Humanitarian Crisis: Conflict in the Global South often leads to mass displacement, loss of lives, and a breakdown of essential services such as healthcare and education. This creates severe humanitarian crises, with vulnerable populations suffering the most.

2. Political Instability: Prolonged conflicts can lead to the collapse of governance structures, weakening state institutions and leaving a power vacuum. This, in turn, can foster political instability, allowing non-state actors to gain influence and exacerbating existing divisions.

3. Economic Underdevelopment: Conflict disrupts economic activities, destroys infrastructure, and hinders foreign investment. The consequences are long-lasting, as countries in the Global South struggle to recover and rebuild their economies, perpetuating a cycle of poverty and underdevelopment.

Conclusion:

Understanding the causes and consequences of conflict in the Global South is vital for students of comparative politics. By delving into the historical, social, and economic factors that contribute to conflict, students can gain a deeper appreciation of the complexities of power and politics in this region. Additionally, recognizing the far-reaching consequences of conflict highlights the urgent need for effective conflict resolution strategies and international cooperation to promote peace, stability, and development in the Global South.

Role of International Intervention in Conflict Resolution

The Role of International Intervention in Conflict Resolution

In the realm of comparative politics, understanding the role of international intervention in conflict resolution is of utmost importance. This subchapter aims to shed light on the various ways in which external actors can contribute to resolving conflicts in the Global South. By examining case studies and analyzing key theories, students will gain a comprehensive understanding of the complexities surrounding international intervention and its impact on conflict resolution.

One key aspect to consider is the motivation behind international intervention. Often, external actors intervene in conflicts within the Global South due to humanitarian concerns, such as protecting civilian populations from violence or ensuring the delivery of essential humanitarian aid. In other instances, intervention may be driven by geopolitical interests, including the desire to establish influence in a particular region or to counterbalance the power of rival states. Exploring these motivations will provide students with a nuanced understanding of the complexities involved in international intervention.

Furthermore, this subchapter will delve into different forms of international intervention. This includes peacekeeping operations, where external actors deploy military forces to maintain peace and stability in conflict-ridden areas. Students will explore the successes and failures of peacekeeping missions, examining cases such as the

United Nations' involvement in the Democratic Republic of the Congo or the African Union's efforts in Somalia.

Additionally, this subchapter will address the role of mediation and diplomacy in conflict resolution. Students will learn about the important role that external mediators play in facilitating negotiations between conflicting parties, aiming to find common ground and reach peaceful settlements. Case studies, such as the Oslo Accords in the Israeli-Palestinian conflict, will be analyzed to provide students with real-world examples of successful mediation efforts.

Furthermore, students will critically analyze the impact of international intervention on the sovereignty and autonomy of conflict-affected states. They will explore the tensions that arise when external actors impose their own visions of peace and stability, often at the expense of the agency of local actors. By examining these dynamics, students will gain a nuanced understanding of the potential pitfalls and ethical dilemmas associated with international intervention.

Overall, this subchapter aims to equip students with the knowledge and critical thinking skills necessary to understand the complexities of international intervention in conflict resolution. By examining different case studies and theories, students will be able to assess the effectiveness and implications of external actors' involvement in conflicts within the Global South.

Case Studies of Post-Conflict Reconstruction in the Global South

Post-conflict reconstruction in the Global South has been a challenging and complex process, as countries grapple with the aftermath of violent conflicts and seek to rebuild their societies. This subchapter aims to provide students with a comparative analysis of key case studies from the Global South, shedding light on the various approaches and strategies employed in post-conflict reconstruction.

One prominent case study is Rwanda, which experienced a devastating genocide in 1994. The reconstruction efforts in Rwanda have focused on rebuilding social cohesion and reconciliation, as well as addressing the root causes of the conflict. The government implemented a combination of grassroots initiatives, such as community-based justice systems and truth and reconciliation commissions, alongside top-down policies aimed at promoting economic growth and stability. By examining the successes and challenges faced in Rwanda, students can gain valuable insights into the complexities of post-conflict reconstruction.

Another compelling case study is Colombia, which has been grappling with a protracted armed conflict for over five decades. The Colombian government has pursued a comprehensive approach to peacebuilding, encompassing political, social, and economic dimensions. This includes the implementation of a peace agreement with the Revolutionary Armed Forces of Colombia (FARC), the establishment of transitional justice mechanisms, and initiatives to address rural development and inequality. By exploring the Colombian experience, students can gain a deeper understanding of the intricacies involved in peacebuilding and the role of political will in driving sustainable change.

Additionally, this subchapter will delve into the case of Mozambique, a country that experienced a civil war that lasted for nearly two decades. Mozambique's post-conflict reconstruction efforts have focused on demobilization and reintegration of combatants, as well as rebuilding infrastructure and promoting economic development. The country has also engaged in external partnerships and international assistance to support its reconstruction process. By analyzing the Mozambican case, students can explore the challenges of rebuilding a war-torn society and the importance of international cooperation in post-conflict reconstruction.

Overall, these case studies highlight the diverse approaches to post-conflict reconstruction in the Global South, showcasing the complexities and successes of different strategies. By examining these cases, students can develop a comparative understanding of the political, social, and economic dynamics that shape post-conflict reconstruction efforts. Through critical analysis of these case studies, students can deepen their knowledge of comparative politics and gain valuable insights into the complexities of power and politics in the Global South.

Chapter 9: Power Dynamics in Regional and International Relations

Regional Organizations in the Global South

In today's interconnected world, regional organizations in the Global South play a crucial role in shaping politics and power dynamics. These organizations act as platforms for collaboration, cooperation, and integration among countries in a specific geographic region. They aim to address common challenges, promote economic development, and enhance political stability within their respective regions. This subchapter will explore the significance and impact of regional organizations in the Global South, providing students with a comprehensive understanding of comparative politics.

One key aspect of regional organizations is their ability to foster regional cooperation and integration. By bringing countries together, these organizations facilitate dialogue and negotiations, leading to the formulation of shared policies and strategies. For instance, the Association of Southeast Asian Nations (ASEAN) has successfully promoted regional economic integration, resulting in the establishment of the ASEAN Economic Community. This has led to the free flow of goods, services, and investments within the region, boosting economic growth and development.

Regional organizations also play a vital role in addressing shared challenges such as security threats, environmental issues, and socio-economic disparities. The African Union (AU) has been instrumental in resolving conflicts and promoting peace and security in the African continent. Through its Peace and Security Council, the AU has deployed peacekeeping missions and mediated in various conflicts, contributing to stability and peacebuilding efforts.

Moreover, regional organizations provide a platform for the Global South to collectively engage with the international community. They amplify the voices and interests of member states on the global stage, enabling them to negotiate from a position of strength. The Group of 77 (G77) and China, for example, represents the interests of developing countries in international forums such as the United Nations, advocating for fair trade, debt relief, and sustainable development.

However, regional organizations also face challenges such as divergent national interests, unequal power dynamics, and the implementation of agreed-upon policies. These organizations must navigate these complexities while ensuring inclusivity, transparency, and accountability in their decision-making processes.

To further comprehend these dynamics, this subchapter will also analyze case studies of regional organizations in different regions of the Global South, such as the Organization of American States (OAS) in Latin America and the Caribbean, the Gulf Cooperation Council (GCC) in the Middle East, and the South Asian Association for Regional Cooperation (SAARC) in South Asia.

By studying regional organizations in the Global South, students will gain valuable insights into the complexities of comparative politics, regional cooperation, and the power dynamics that shape the contemporary world order. This knowledge will equip them with a comprehensive understanding of the challenges and opportunities faced by countries in the Global South, enabling them to critically analyze and contribute to the field of global politics.

Power Struggles and Alliances in the Global South

In the complex realm of global politics, power struggles and alliances play a critical role in shaping the dynamics of the Global South. This subchapter aims to provide students of comparative politics with an insightful understanding of these dynamics, exploring the causes, consequences, and complexities of power struggles and alliances within this diverse region.

The Global South refers to a group of countries primarily located in Africa, Latin America, and Asia, which share common challenges related to economic development, governance, and social issues. Despite their shared struggles, these countries are marked by significant diversity in terms of history, culture, and political systems. Understanding the power dynamics and alliances within this context is crucial to comprehending the complexities of global politics.

Power struggles in the Global South are often born out of historical legacies, socio-economic disparities, and competing interests. Historical colonialism and post-colonialism have left lasting imprints on power structures, with former colonizers often maintaining influence or seeking to reassert control. Within these countries, power struggles can arise between different political factions, ethnic groups, or social classes, each vying for control and resources.

At the same time, alliances are formed to consolidate power, promote economic development, and address common challenges. These alliances can take various forms, including regional blocs, economic partnerships, or even informal networks. The Association of Southeast Asian Nations (ASEAN), the African Union (AU), and the Mercado

Común del Sur (MERCOSUR) are prominent examples of regional alliances in the Global South.

Understanding power struggles and alliances in the Global South requires analyzing their consequences both domestically and internationally. Domestically, power struggles can lead to political instability, economic stagnation, and social unrest. On the other hand, alliances can provide opportunities for economic cooperation, regional integration, and collective bargaining power in global forums.

Moreover, the influence of the Global South has been growing in international politics, with emerging powers such as China, India, and Brazil seeking to challenge the dominance of traditional powers. The alliances formed within the Global South can amplify their influence on global issues such as climate change, trade, and human rights.

In conclusion, power struggles and alliances in the Global South are essential factors in shaping the region's political landscape. By understanding these dynamics, students of comparative politics can gain a comprehensive perspective on the complex power structures and challenges faced by countries in the Global South. Moreover, the consequences of power struggles and alliances have far-reaching implications, both domestically and internationally. Studying these dynamics is crucial for anyone seeking to navigate the intricacies of global politics and better comprehend the evolving dynamics of power in the Global South.

Role of Developing Countries in International Organizations

Developing countries play a crucial role in international organizations, shaping global politics and exerting their influence in various ways. This subchapter explores the significance of developing countries in international organizations, focusing on their role in shaping global policies, promoting their interests, and addressing the unique challenges they face.

In the realm of global politics, developing countries are often seen as the voice of the Global South. They represent a significant majority of the world's population and possess a diverse range of cultures, resources, and perspectives. As such, they bring a different lens to global issues, challenging the dominance of Western powers and advocating for the rights and aspirations of their own people. This subchapter will delve into how developing countries have successfully used international organizations as platforms to amplify their voices and influence global decision-making processes.

One of the key roles of developing countries in international organizations is to promote their own interests. They actively engage in negotiations, alliances, and partnerships to secure favorable outcomes for their economies, societies, and populations. This subchapter will explore how developing countries have used their collective bargaining power to push for fair trade practices, debt relief, and technology transfer, among other issues. It will also discuss the challenges they face in these processes, such as power imbalances and the influence of developed countries.

Furthermore, this subchapter will address the unique challenges that developing countries face in international organizations. These challenges include limited resources, capacity building needs, and the struggle to balance national interests with global responsibilities. The content will explore how developing countries navigate these challenges and seek to address them through collective action, regional cooperation, and strategic alliances.

This subchapter will provide students with a comprehensive understanding of the role of developing countries in international organizations. By examining case studies and real-world examples, students will gain insights into the power dynamics at play, the strategies employed by developing countries, and the impact of their participation in global decision-making processes. It will encourage critical thinking and analysis, enabling students to evaluate the effectiveness and limitations of developing countries' influence in international organizations.

Overall, this subchapter aims to equip students with the knowledge and tools to comprehend the dynamic role of developing countries in international organizations. By understanding the complexities and nuances of this topic, students can develop a deeper understanding of comparative politics and contribute to discussions on global governance and power dynamics.

Case Studies of Global South's Influence in International Relations

In this subchapter, we delve into the fascinating world of international relations and explore how the Global South has emerged as a significant force in shaping the global political landscape. We will examine several case studies that highlight the growing influence of countries in the Global South, providing students with a comprehensive understanding of the dynamics at play in international politics.

Our first case study takes us to Brazil, a rising power in the Global South. We analyze Brazil's role in the United Nations Security Council and its efforts to promote international peace and security. By engaging in peacekeeping missions and advocating for the rights of developing nations, Brazil has successfully challenged traditional power dynamics and asserted its influence on the global stage. We also explore Brazil's active role in regional organizations such as Mercosur, showcasing the country's commitment to regional integration and cooperation.

Next, we shift our focus to India, a prominent player in South Asia and beyond. Through a detailed analysis of India's foreign policy, we examine the country's pursuit of strategic partnerships and its efforts to enhance its soft power. We explore India's diplomatic approach in addressing regional conflicts, such as the Kashmir dispute, and how it has leveraged its economic and cultural influence to build strong alliances. Students will gain valuable insights into the complexities of India's foreign policy and the challenges it faces in balancing its regional and global aspirations.

Moving on, we explore the role of South Africa in shaping international relations. We examine South Africa's journey from apartheid to democracy and its subsequent emergence as a leader in the African continent. Through an analysis of the country's role in the African Union and its engagement with regional conflicts, such as the Zimbabwe crisis, students will gain a deeper understanding of South Africa's pursuit of peace, stability, and economic development in Africa.

Lastly, we investigate the influence of China, a rising global power, on the international stage. We delve into China's economic diplomacy, its engagement with regional organizations such as ASEAN, and its ambitious Belt and Road Initiative. Students will gain insights into China's growing influence in Africa and Latin America and its evolving role as a major player in global governance.

Through these case studies, students will develop a nuanced understanding of the Global South's increasing importance in international relations. By analyzing the diverse strategies and challenges faced by countries in the Global South, students will be equipped with the knowledge to critically analyze and contribute to the field of comparative politics.

Chapter 10: Conclusion and Future Perspectives

Summary of Key Findings

In this subchapter, we will provide a comprehensive summary of the key findings from our comparative study on power and politics in the Global South. This book aims to equip students with a deeper understanding of the political dynamics in various countries across the Global South and explore the complexities of comparative politics.

1. Diversity of Political Systems: One of the major findings of our study is the immense diversity of political systems in the Global South. From democratic to authoritarian regimes, each country has its unique political structure shaped by historical, cultural, and economic factors.

2. Power Dynamics: We discovered that power dynamics in the Global South are often influenced by factors such as colonial legacies, ethnic and religious divisions, and economic disparities. This has resulted in complex power struggles between different groups within societies.

3. Role of Global Actors: Our research highlights the significant role played by global actors in shaping the political landscape of the Global South. We found that international organizations, powerful nations, and multinational corporations often exert influence on domestic politics, sometimes leading to tensions and conflicts.

4. Challenges to Democracy: Despite the global trend towards democratization, we found that many countries in the Global South face challenges in consolidating and sustaining democratic systems. Issues such as corruption, weak institutions, and limited civic participation pose obstacles to democratic governance.

5. Socioeconomic Factors: Our study reveals the strong link between socioeconomic factors and political stability. We found that countries with higher levels of inequality, poverty, and unemployment tend to experience more political unrest and instability.

6. Regional Dynamics: The Global South is not a homogenous entity, and our research highlights the importance of regional dynamics in shaping political outcomes. We analyzed regional organizations, alliances, and conflicts to better understand the interactions between countries within a specific region.

7. Role of Civil Society: Lastly, our study emphasizes the crucial role played by civil society in promoting democratic values, advocating for human rights, and holding governments accountable. We found that vibrant civil society organizations contribute to a more inclusive and participatory political environment.

By summarizing these key findings, our aim is to provide students with a comprehensive overview of the political landscape in the Global South. This knowledge will enable them to critically analyze and understand the complexities of comparative politics, fostering a deeper appreciation for the dynamics of power and politics in different societies.

Implications for Students and Future Scholars

As students of comparative politics, it is essential to understand the implications of power and politics in the global South. This subchapter delves into the various ways in which the study of this subject can significantly impact students and future scholars. By examining the intricacies of power dynamics and political structures in the global South, students gain a deeper understanding of the complexities that shape societies and governments in this region.

First and foremost, studying power and politics in the global South provides students with a comprehensive framework for analyzing and comparing political systems. By exploring diverse case studies from countries such as Brazil, India, and South Africa, students can identify commonalities and differences in political ideologies, institutions, and policies. This comparative approach allows for a nuanced understanding of the unique challenges and opportunities faced by nations in the global South, fostering critical thinking skills and analytical abilities.

Furthermore, this subchapter highlights the significance of studying power dynamics for future scholars. By delving into the complexities of power structures in the global South, students are equipped with the tools necessary to conduct their own research and contribute to the field of comparative politics. The knowledge gained from this study can inform future scholars' work on topics such as democratization, political economy, social movements, and governance in the global South.

Another implication for students and future scholars is the insight gained into the impact of power and politics on development and social change. The global South is often characterized by vast economic disparities, social inequalities, and struggles for human rights. By examining the role of power in shaping these realities, students can gain a deeper understanding of the challenges faced by these societies. This understanding can inform future scholars' efforts to propose innovative solutions and policies that promote inclusive development and social justice.

Lastly, studying power and politics in the global South encourages students to adopt a global perspective and challenges ethnocentric biases. By engaging with diverse case studies and perspectives, students are exposed to different cultural, historical, and socio-political contexts. This exposure fosters empathy, cultural sensitivity, and a broader understanding of the interconnectedness of the global political landscape.

In conclusion, the study of power and politics in the global South provides students and future scholars with invaluable insights and skills. By analyzing political systems, understanding power dynamics, and examining the impacts on development and social change, students can contribute to the field of comparative politics and work towards a more equitable world. The implications of this study reach far beyond the classroom, empowering students to become agents of positive change in the global South and beyond.

Future Challenges and Opportunities in Power and Politics in the Global South

As students of comparative politics, it is crucial to understand the dynamic nature of power and politics in the Global South. The Global South, comprising developing and emerging nations across Africa, Asia, and Latin America, presents unique challenges and opportunities that shape the future of power and politics in this region.

One of the major challenges in the Global South is the persistence of corruption. Corruption undermines democratic institutions, hinders economic development, and perpetuates inequality. Students studying comparative politics should explore innovative solutions to combat corruption and promote transparency and accountability in governance. This could include strengthening anti-corruption measures, encouraging civic participation, and fostering a culture of integrity within political systems.

Another significant challenge in the Global South is the rise of authoritarianism and the erosion of democratic values. Many countries in this region have experienced a trend towards the concentration of power in the hands of a few individuals or ruling parties. Students should critically analyze the causes and consequences of this phenomenon and explore strategies to promote democratic governance, protect human rights, and ensure checks and balances within political systems.

Furthermore, the Global South faces unique environmental challenges that have profound political implications. Climate change, deforestation, and resource scarcity are not only environmental issues but also political and social challenges. Students must understand the complex interplay between power, politics, and environmental issues and explore avenues for sustainable development, renewable energy, and climate change mitigation in the Global South.

Despite these challenges, the Global South also presents numerous opportunities for positive change. Many countries in this region have experienced significant economic growth and are emerging as global players. Students should explore how this economic transformation can be harnessed to promote inclusive development, reduce poverty, and address social inequalities. They should study successful case studies and learn from the experiences of countries that have effectively leveraged their economic growth to improve the lives of their citizens.

Moreover, the Global South is characterized by its rich cultural diversity and vibrant civil societies. Students should explore how this diversity can be harnessed to build inclusive and participatory political systems that respect and empower marginalized communities. They should also study the role of civil society organizations in advocating for social justice, promoting human rights, and amplifying marginalized voices.

In conclusion, the future of power and politics in the Global South presents both challenges and opportunities. As students of comparative politics, it is crucial to critically analyze and understand these dynamics. By exploring innovative solutions to combat corruption, promote democracy, address environmental challenges, and leverage economic growth for inclusive development, students can contribute towards shaping a more equitable and sustainable future in the Global South.

Final Thoughts and Recommendations for Further Study

As we conclude our journey through the intricate world of power and politics in the Global South, it is essential to reflect on the knowledge and insights gained. This subchapter serves as a synthesis of our findings and offers recommendations for further study, specifically tailored to students interested in the field of comparative politics.

Throughout this book, we have explored the diverse political landscapes of the Global South, recognizing the complex interplay between power dynamics, socio-economic factors, and historical context. We have examined case studies from Latin America, Africa, Asia, and the Middle East, shedding light on the unique challenges and opportunities faced by these regions.

One overarching recommendation for further study is to delve deeper into the specific political systems and structures of countries within the Global South. Focusing on comparative analysis, students can explore the similarities and differences between various political ideologies, such as socialism, communism, and democracy, as they manifest in different contexts. This will provide a more nuanced understanding of the political landscape and its impact on governance, development, and societal dynamics.

Moreover, an exploration of the role of international actors in the Global South is crucial. Students should examine the influence of global powers, international organizations, and multilateral agreements on the political dynamics of these regions. Understanding the motivations and agendas of external actors will shed light on the power dynamics and potential sources of conflict or cooperation within the Global South.

Furthermore, incorporating interdisciplinary approaches can enhance students' understanding of power and politics in the Global South. By integrating perspectives from sociology, anthropology, economics, and history, students can gain a comprehensive understanding of the complex factors that shape political systems and processes. This interdisciplinary approach will enable students to develop a holistic understanding of the Global South and its political challenges.

Lastly, we encourage students to engage with local communities and immerse themselves in the realities of the Global South. Participating in internships, fieldwork, or study abroad programs can provide firsthand experiences and insights into the political dynamics of these regions. Building connections with local scholars and activists will enrich students' understanding and offer opportunities for collaboration and mutual learning.

In conclusion, the study of power and politics in the Global South is a fascinating and vital field for students of comparative politics. By delving deeper into specific political systems, exploring the role of international actors, adopting interdisciplinary approaches, and engaging with local communities, students can contribute to a more nuanced understanding of the political dynamics of these regions. As the world becomes increasingly interconnected, it is essential to comprehend the unique challenges and opportunities faced by countries in the Global South. Through continued study and engagement, students have the opportunity to contribute to positive change and shape the future of global politics.